LIFE'S LESSONS

589/3000

Published for
BOB TIMBERLAKE, INC. *and*
THE AVENIR FOUNDATION *by*
GOOSEPEN STUDIO & PRESS
Conover, North Carolina

"The Lord is happiest with his children at play."
— CHARLES KURALT

LIFE'S LESSONS

Lines of Wisdom from a Faithful Stream

Bob Timberlake & Mark Erwin

Copyright © 2012
by Bob Timberlake
and Mark Erwin.

All rights reserved.

Designed, set in
Brioso Pro, and published
by Nathan W. Moehlmann
Goosepen Studio & Press.
www.GoosepenPress.com

Printed on acid-free paper
and bound by Friesens
in Altona, Manitoba, Canada.

ISBN 978-0-9793631-6-0

www.BobTimberlake.com
www.erenvine.com

*With special gratitude
to Sherry Sink
for her wonderful help
and encouragement.*

~

In honor of the life and legacy of

THE REVEREND BILLY GRAHAM

and in memory and honor of

ALL WHO HAVE SACRIFICED
FOR THE FREEDOMS
OF OUR NATION

~

Contents

DEDICATION 5

FOREWORDS *Bob Timberlake & Mark Erwin* 9

GOOD HAIR DAYS 19

THE CHEROKEE BRAVE 33

HIS NAME WAS BILL 47

THE KING, THE BOULDER, AND THE PEASANT 63

A BLIND MAN'S PROFESSION 79

ONE TOUCH OF NATURE 91

LIST OF ILLUSTRATIONS 111

Forewords

~ Bob ~

Mark and I met many years ago on a hunting trip. Among some twenty extremely interesting folks hailing from all over the United States – most were national leaders of various sorts – I had the fortunate opportunity to sit by Mark at the game table one evening. We started swapping stories about family and discovered in each other a common sense of cultural heritage, including a devotion to God, family, friends, and country, and a passion for the sportsman's life of hunting and fishing, conservation, and dogs. We found in each other a kindred soul – due not least to our mutual penchant for jotting down and sharing stories, sayings, and bits of wisdom, sometimes our own, often those of others, whether we read them, hear them, or receive them third-hand, smoothed and polished from being passed along. Mark and I continued our conversation later on the porch, and it has continued to this day, through many more hunts and get-togethers and through the many lines of wisdom we have cast back and forth. In celebration of our friendship, family, faith, and the generations to come, we would like to share some of the thoughts, feelings, and the lessons of life that we have shared between ourselves.

> Life is too short to spend time with negative folks.
> Enjoy life and try to make the lives of those you meet
> happier. Be positive, as my friend, Mark, is.
> "We can't do everything for everyone,"
> as Confucius has said, "but everyone
> can do something for someone."
> Now that seems like a good
> life lesson to me.

I'm the product of the people, places, and things that have made me what I am today. We are all woven, each of us, into a distinct fabric not just from parents and grandparents, but school teachers, preachers, Scout leaders, Sunday School teachers, neighbors, brothers, sisters, and friends. I would have never made it to manhood without the many "aunts" and "uncles" of color and white, famous and unknown, who took me in and "raised me up." Each of us is unique because everything we ever do and everyone we ever meet are a part of what we are today. I also happen to believe that it's not our talents so much but our choices in life that make us whatever it is we become. As General Norman Schwarzkopf said, "The truth of the matter is that you always know the right thing to do. The hard part is doing it."

Other than family, the three folks who have influenced my life the most, helping me with the hard part of doing the right thing, are Dr. Howard Wilkinson, who was more than just my Methodist minister in Lexington when I was a teenager. He was my hunting and fishing buddy, my friend and mentor, who lived in the spirit of the Lord both in the pulpit and the duck blind. He married Kay and me and all of our three children. He went on to be chaplain at Duke University and

"We are all woven, each of us, into a distinct fabric."

— *Bob Timberlake*

"What is a friend? A single soul dwelling in two bodies."

— Aristotle

president of Greensboro College. Dr. Hal Warlick, another Methodist minister, became a dear friend later in my life, as did his sweet wife, Diane. One of the best preachers in the country, Hal addresses his congregations with the Bible in one hand and a newspaper in the other. Hal's sermons and our talks reinvigorate me and rekindle my creativity and faith in the positive, while bringing me down to earth. All you have to do is ask one of the thousands of students, friends, just folks, and associates who have heard him preach at Harvard, Yale, Furman, High Point University, and Vanderbilt and at his church, Blowing Rock Methodist, in the North Carolina mountains. Hal is mostly retired now, but spends his summers as acting minister for this tiny, historic church, which overflows in the summer months. Oftentimes, the doors will be open, fans turning cool air, and tents and speakers set up outside to accommodate the folks who didn't arrive thirty minutes early to sing "The Church in the Wildwood." My dear friend, Mark Erwin, has been another precious influence on my life. Mark is a very successful, happy, smart, energetic, and downright nice guy. (Nice people do make it sometimes, and Mark has served as a United States Ambassador and close friend and confidant to many of our country's political movers and shakers.) A true friend does something for you before you know you need it done, and of his many gifts to me is *Life's Lessons*. As I have believed for many years, you have to be happy with yourself to make others happy, and I hope our book will inspire others to enjoy life and be happy.

— *Bob Timberlake*

"We should spend our time with those who inspire us to be more and better." — *Mark Erwin*

~ Mark ~

We live our lives in chapters, punctuated by inexplicable, sometimes extraordinary, even magical defining moments. I sometimes wonder whether the story of our lives is already written before we are born. This would help explain some of the strange parts I have been allowed to play and of the almost mystical circumstances of time and place which have allowed me to be a part of what might be a grand plan. From a somewhat discouraging beginning my life has been a wonderful pageant of opportunities and experiences.

My dear friend, Bob Timberlake, has been a favorite artist since my wife, Joan, and I began buying his works in the 1970s. We both love his understanding and interpretation of nature's beauty. It was not until years later that Bob and I were brought together – a magical alignment – at Tobacco Stick Lodge on the Eastern Shore of Maryland. Tobacco Stick was a hunting lodge owned by Tommy and Barbara Boggs, my dear friends and now Bob's, as well. The small gathering included many prominent United States leaders. I picked Bob as my dinner seatmate, and as we shared our stories, there was an instant bond that has flourished over the years.

> I have learned the most important things in life
> are not things; they are faith in God and people,
> the former who loves us unconditionally
> and the latter – family and friends – who have
> cared enough to love me, correct me, befriend me,
> advise me, and mentor me along the way.

HILLARY CLINTON HAD IT RIGHT WHEN SHE SAID,
"IT TAKES A VILLAGE TO RAISE A CHILD."
TODAY, I WOULD ADD, IT TAKES FRIENDS AND FAMILY
TO NURTURE A PERSON WHO WILL MAKE A DIFFERENCE.

DURING QUIET TIMES – in church or in bed in the middle of the night or in a crowd where I am anonymous – I jot down thoughts of faith, inspiration, and wisdom. Sometimes I make a note of a pithy saying that I've heard or read. When I sent Bob a rough draft of a book I was working on, he loved it and suggested we collaborate on the project. We both had been collecting quotes and inspirational thoughts about life for many years. This book combines his incredible art with the essence of our shared love of God, history, family, friends, art, and the sporting life. The sources of the quotations range from founding fathers to a Bermudian taxi driver. Bob and I have made every effort to attribute the quotations properly, though many were stashed away without thought of their ever appearing in a book of our own. In a few instances, we have had to rely on the words of Joe DiScala, a dear friend, who said years ago, "We never actually own anything. We're merely given the right to take care of a few things for a while." I hope you enjoy.

— *Mark Erwin*

Good Hair Days

There once was a woman who woke up one morning, looked in the mirror, and noticed she had only three hairs on her head. "Well," she said, "I think I'll braid my hair today." So she did and she had a wonderful day.

The next day she woke up, looked in the mirror, and saw that she had only two hairs on her head. "Hmm," she said, "I think I'll part my hair down the middle today." So she did and she had a grand day.

The next day she woke up, looked in the mirror, and noticed that she had only one hair on her head. "Well," she said, "today I'm going to wear my hair in a pony tail." So she did and she had a fun, fun day.

The next day she woke up, looked in the mirror, and noticed that there wasn't a single hair on her head. "Yea!" she exclaimed, "I don't have to fix my hair today!"

— *Shared with Mark by his daughter, Jennifer Erwin*

"WE ARE ALL AS YOUNG AS WE DREAM AND AS OLD AS OUR CYNICISM."

— *Tony Compolo*

"A smile is the best way to improve your looks." — *Andy Rooney*

"JOY is not in things; it is in US."   — Richard Wagner

"You must learn day by day, year by year, to broaden your horizon. The more things you love, the more you are interested in, the more you enjoy, the more you are indignant about – the more you have left when anything happens."

— Ethel Barrymore

"If you cut the sycamore down, you'll never know how high it will grow."

— James Allen

"I've learned that you can tell a lot about a person by the way he or she handles these three things: a rainy day, lost luggage, and tangled Christmas tree lights."

— Maya Angelou

"Smile when you pick up the phone. The caller will hear it in your voice."

— Read in Forbes Magazine

"Hitch your wagon to a star."   — Emerson

"Life is what you make of it,
ALWAYS has been,
ALWAYS will be."

— Grandma Moses

"We don't stop playing because we grow old,
we grow old because we stop playing."

— C. Wyatt Runyan

**"Promise me you'll always remember:
you're braver than you believe,
and stronger than you seem,
and smarter than you think."**

— Christopher Robin to Pooh

"Reasonable people adapt themselves to the world. Unreasonable people attempt to adapt the world to themselves. All progress, therefore, depends on unreasonable people."

— George Bernard Shaw

"Boredom is a matter of choice, not circumstance."

— Gustav Stickley

"First say to yourself **what you would be**;
and then do what you have to do."

— Epictetus

"Don't part with your illusions;
when they are gone you may still exist,
but you have ceased to live."

— Mark Twain

"Go confidently in the direction of your dreams! Live the life you've imagined."

— Henry David Thoreau

"If we all did the things we are capable of doing, we would literally astound ourselves."

— Thomas Edison

"Ten thousand flowers in spring, the moon in autumn, a cool breeze in summer, snow in winter. If your mind isn't clouded by unnecessary things, this is the best season of your life."

— Wu-men

"How old would you be if you didn't know how old you are?"

— Satchel Page

"Pretend to be happy long enough and one day you will wake up and realize you can hardly tell it from the real thing."

— Mattie W. Hamrick (1919–2011)

"From my mother came this bit of wisdom. As a child I grew up feeling I was the homeliest girl in school. I must have acted and looked so sad, but one day my mother asked, 'What is wrong?' I told her, 'You make me feel guilty and make me sad.' And her reply was 'As long as you live you must realize how rich you are — I am a seamstress and you have all the nice clothes, you have a nice warm bed, and Grandpa supplies all the best food from his fields of vegetables. If you don't remember anything else, just remember how much joy, peace of mind, love, and happiness come from making yourself find it.' To this day, I've found some of all."

— *Mattie W. Hamrick (1919–2011)*

"**The more you praise and celebrate your life, the more there is in life to celebrate.**"

— *Oprah Winfrey*

"Every blade of grass has its angel that bends over it and whispers, *grow, grow*."

— *The Talmud*

"No matter where
you make your nest,
it's how you feather it
that makes the difference."

— Bob Timberlake

"Accept that some days you're the pigeon,
and some days you're the statue."

— Heard on a hunt at Webb Farm

"I believe there is a vast difference between change and chance. . . . The longer you do not believe you are deserving of the benefits that come with positive thought and action, the longer you stay stuck. Draw the line in the sand, turn around, and face what is holding you back."

— *James Allen*

"Just when the caterpillar thought the world was over . . . it became a butterfly."

— *One of Bob's favorite sayings*

"Life is just a bowl of cherries." — *DeSylva & Brown*

"A truly happy person is one who can enjoy the scenery on a detour."

— *Seen on a sign on a detour*

"May the sun bring you new energy by day.
May the moon softly restore you by night.
May the rain wash away your worries.
May the breeze blow new strength into your being.
May you walk gently through the world and know
its beauty all the days of your life."

— *Apache Blessing*

The Cherokee Brave

A Cherokee father was required to take his young son into the forest, blindfold him, and leave him. The boy was required to sit on a stump the whole night and not remove the blindfold until the rays of the sun shone through it. He could not cry out for help. If he survived the night, he would be a man. The father could not share his own experience, because each must come into manhood himself. The boy was naturally terrified. Wild beasts were surely all around. Finally, after a terrifying night the sun appeared, and the boy removed his blindfold. It was then he discovered his father sitting next to him. He had been at watch the entire night long.

> **"The most powerful forces on earth are unseen: gravity, wisdom, hate, love, and most powerful of all, God."**
>
> — *Mark Erwin*

> "The will of God will never take you where the Grace of God will not protect you."
>
> — *Steve Eason*

"Jesus left us his unseen spirit." — Doug Coe

"Keep your honor code between you and God;
no matter who's not looking, God always is."

— Caroline Myss

"It is impossible to account for the creation
of the universe without the agency of a Supreme Being."

— George Washington

"Heaven is under our feet, as well as over our heads."

— Henry David Thoreau

"I have been driven many times to my knees by the overwhelming conviction that I had nowhere else to go. My own wisdom, and that of all about me, seemed insufficient for that day."

— Abraham Lincoln

"There are limits to humans, and beyond these limits
only God can work. Then comes God's Grace."

— Mark Erwin

36

"America was founded by people who believed that God was their rock of safety. I recognize we must be cautious in claiming that God is on our side, but I think it's all right to keep asking if we're on His side."

— Ronald Reagan

"And there are angels living amongst us."

— Bob Timberlake

"If a sparrow cannot fall to the ground without God's notice, is it probable that an empire can rise without His aid?"

— Benjamin Franklin

"I say again, don't let someone tell you you're weak because you don't agree with everything somebody else does. And don't let somebody [say] you're not a good Christian because your views on certain issues don't fit the party line. . . . Remind them that all have sinned and fallen short of God's glory and all of us see through the glass darkly."

— William J. Clinton

"Preach the gospel wherever you go, and if you have to – use words."

— St. Francis of Assisi

"If a single man achieves
the highest kind of love,
it will be sufficient to neutralize
the hate of millions."

— *Mahatma Gandhi*

"I always have said, and always will say, that the studious perusal of the sacred Volume will make better citizens, better fathers, and better husbands. . . . I hold the precepts of Jesus as delivered by Himself to be the most pure, benevolent, and sublime which have ever been preached to man."

— *Thomas Jefferson*

"Faith was not meant to be divided." — *Jennifer Erwin*

"Have you ever wondered why God put you on earth, what is the purpose and meaning of life? It is to know Him and to know His love."

— *Billy Graham*

"Cities crumble, civilizations come and go, and religions die because they are all created by us, but faith in a power greater than mankind lives on forever."

— *Mark Erwin*

"I WILL HONOR CHRISTMAS
IN MY HEART, AND TRY
TO KEEP IT ALL THE YEAR."

— *Charles Dickens*

"We should be glad God doesn't give us everything we ask for."

— Missy Highsmith, Mark's daughter

"When God takes something from your grasp,
He's not punishing you, but merely opening
your hands to receive something else."

— A beautiful sermon

"I love the snow, the quietness, and the beauty — IT'S A GIFT from God. I become a child again."

— Bob Timberlake

"Man's accidents are God's purposes."

— Sophia A. Hawthorne

"God accepts us the way we are,
but loves us too much to leave us that way."

— Tony Zeiss

Just Remember,

Noah was a drinker and Abraham was old.
Isaac was a daydreamer and Jacob was a liar.
Isaiah preached naked and Jonah ran from God.
Gideon was afraid and Sampson was a womanizer.
Job went bankrupt and John the Baptist ate bugs.
The Samaritan woman was divorced, more than once.
Joseph was abused and Moses had a stuttering problem.
Elijah was suicidal and David had an affair and was a murderer.
Rahab was a prostitute and Jeremiah and Timothy were too young.
Zaccheus was tiny and Paul was too religious and Lazarus was dead!
Peter denied Christ three times and the Disciples fell asleep while praying.

God Needs You Too.

— *Heard at the National Prayer Breakfast*

"Live in such a way that those who know you, but don't know Christ, will come to know Christ because they know you."

— *Steve Eason*

The most compelling evidence of all that Jesus was a woman:

1) He had to feed a crowd at a moment's notice when there was no food. 2) He kept trying to get a message to a bunch of men who just didn't get it. 3) Even when he was dead, He had to get up since there was more work to do.

— *Heard in church*

"**The love of Christ knows no boundaries.** The love of Christ extends beyond all thoughts and tongues where it reigns without rival. We can only experience this reign by uniting our thankful hearts to Christ's. When we unite with this constant flame, we find love, but not necessarily safety, ease, or comfort. Even within the boundless love of Christ there is suffering. With the love of Christ as our constant guide, we are led through the manmade barriers of barbwire and provided with a boundless, panoramic view where we are aware of weakness and suffering, but granted peace and power."

— *Carter Ellis, Bob's granddaughter*

"Thus am I, a feather on the breath of God."

— *Hildegard von Bingen*

"Before you go to bed, give your troubles to God. He will be up all night anyway."

— *From a sign painted by Laurie Sherrell*

His Name Was Bill

His name was Bill. He was in his early twenties and had wild hair, and he wore a T-shirt with holes in it, blue jeans, and no shoes. This was literally his wardrobe for his entire four years of college. He was a brilliant student, but kind of eccentric. A very, very bright young man. He had become a Christian while attending college.

Across the street from campus was a church with a very well-dressed, very conservative congregation. They wanted to develop a ministry to the students, but were not sure how to go about it.

One Sunday, Bill decided to visit the church. He walked in shoeless, with his jeans, T-shirt, and wild hair. The service had already begun, but Bill started down the aisle looking for a seat. The church was completely packed and he couldn't find a seat. By then people were looking a bit uncomfortable, but no one said anything. Bill got closer and closer to the pulpit, and when he realized there were no seats, he just squatted down right on the carpet.

About that time, the minister realized that from way at the back of the church, a deacon was slowly making his way toward Bill. Now the deacon was in his eighties and he had silver-gray hair and a three-piece suit. A godly man, very elegant, very dignified, very courtly. He walked with a cane. As he started toward the boy, everyone was saying to themselves that you can't blame him for what he was going to do. How could you expect a man of his age and background to understand some college kid sitting on the floor in church?

It took a long time for the man to reach the boy. The minister had fallen silent. Not a breath could be heard over the clicking of the man's cane. All eyes were focused on him. And now they saw this elderly man drop his cane on the floor. With great difficulty, the old man lowered himself and sat down next to Bill and worshipped with him so Bill wouldn't be alone.

Everyone was choked up with emotion. The congregation grew heavy with emotion, and when the minister gained control, he said, "What I'm about to preach – you will never remember. What you have just seen – you will never forget. Be careful how you live. You may be the only Bible some people will ever read."

— *Shared by Tara Snow*

"Flowers leave some of their fragrance in the hand that bestows them."

— *Chinese proverb*

"If you think there is nothing you can do to make a difference then pray to God that He give you an assignment."

— *Mark Erwin*

"When it comes to fellowship, size matters. Smaller is better. You can worship with a crowd, but you cannot fellowship with one. Jesus ministered in the context of a small group of disciples."
— Doug Coe

"If you want to witness a miracle, be one to someone."

— Mark Erwin

"Who, being loved, is poor?"

— Oscar Wilde

*"If you are bold for the poor,
you will be magnificent to the Lord."*

— Mark Erwin

"We in America won the geography lottery.
We are not any better – only different."

— *Mark Erwin*

At college a professor gave us a pop quiz. I was fine until I read the last question: "What is the first name of the janitor?" I had seen the janitor several times, but how would I know his name? I handed in my paper without answering the question. I asked if the last question would count toward our quiz grade. The professor said, "In your life you will meet many people. All are significant and deserve your attention, even if all you do is smile and say hello." I learned that his name was Jack, and he had a wife and three little children.

— *Bob Timberlake*

"Be not forgetful to entertain strangers for thereby some have entertained angels unawares."

— *Hebrews 13:2*

"God will not look you over for medals, degrees, or diplomas, but for scars."

— *Elbert Hubbard*

"Do a good deed for someone else every day."

— *Taxi driver in Bermuda, 1991*

> "Consider the trees.
> The largest give more shade,
> more fruit, more oxygen, more wood.
> From the largest more is expected,
> but from the small
> an equal portion will be expected."
>
> — Mark Erwin

> "To be happy at home is the ultimate result of all ambition
> – the end to which all enterprise and labour tends."
>
> — Samuel Johnson

A little girl named Liz was suffering from a rare disease. Her only chance of recovery appeared to be a blood transfusion from her five year old brother, who had miraculously survived the same disease and had developed the antibodies needed to combat the illness. The doctor explained this to her little brother and asked if he would be willing to give his blood to his sister. He hesitated for only a moment before taking a deep breath and saying, "Yes, I'll do it if it will save her." As the transfusion progressed, he lay in bed next to his sister and smiled, seeing the color returning to her cheek. Then his face grew pale and his smile faded. He looked up at the doctor and asked with a trembling voice, "Will I start to die right away?" The little boy had misunderstood the doctor and thought he was going to give his sister all of his blood.

> "Other things may change us,
> but we start and end with the family."
>
> — Anthony Brandt

"This is the true nature of home
 – it is the place of Peace."

— John Ruskin

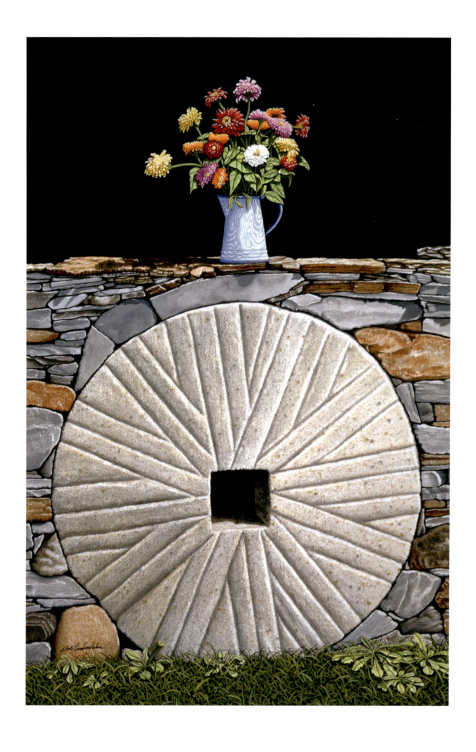

"Love cures people – both the ones who give it
and the ones who receive it."

— Karl Menninger

"I love the little children, and it is not a slight thing
when they, who are fresh from God, love us."

— Charles Dickens

"Love all of your children equally – care for them
based upon their individual needs."

— Mark Erwin

"All loves should be simply stepping stones to the love of God."

— Plato

"As my grandfather Casper Hill Timberlake once said to me,
'People hear what you say, see what you do, and believe what they see.'"

— Dan Timberlake

"One of the most influential lessons imparted to me by a mentor
has been that the best answer to a question is another question."

— Carter Ellis

"Being kind is more important than being right." — H. Jackson Brown

"If you can't be kind, at least have the decency to be vague."

— Jerry Seinfeld

"Always keep your words soft and sweet, just in case you have to eat them."

— Andy Rooney

A TEN YEAR OLD BOY ENTERED A HOTEL coffee shop and sat at a table. The waitress put a glass of water in front of him. "How much is an ice cream sundae?" he asked. "Fifty cents," replied the waitress. The little boy pulled his hand out of his pocket and studied the coins in it. "How much is a plain dish of ice cream?" he inquired. "Thirty-five cents," she brusquely replied. The little boy again counted his coins. "I'll have the plain ice cream," he said. The waitress brought the ice cream, put the bill on the table, and walked away. The boy finished the ice cream and left. When the waitress came back, she began to cry as she wiped down the table. There, placed neatly beside the empty dish, were four dimes and two nickels. You see, he couldn't have the sundae because he had to have enough left to leave her a tip.

"ONE OF THE DEEP SECRETS OF LIFE IS THAT ALL THAT IS REALLY WORTH DOING IS WHAT WE DO FOR OTHERS."

— Lewis Carroll

"Pick your friends carefully; they reflect your character."

— *Gustav Vinroot*

"We unwittingly become better for having great friends."

— *Mark Erwin*

"Friends are the family you get to pick."

— *Mark Erwin*

"A successful marriage requires falling in love many times with the same person."

— *Mignon McLaughlin*

"Love seems the swiftest, but it is the slowest of all growths. No man or woman really knows what perfect love is until they have been married a quarter of a century."

— Mark Twain

"A love unexpressed is only an illusion."

— Sunday School lesson

"Love doesn't make the world go round. Love is what makes the ride worthwhile."

— Franklin P. Jones

"Love seems the swiftest, but it is the slowest of all growths. No man or woman really knows what perfect love is until they have been married a quarter of a century."

— Mark Twain

"A love unexpressed is only an illusion."

— Sunday School lesson

"Love doesn't make the world go round. Love is what makes the ride worthwhile."

— Franklin P. Jones

The King, the Boulder, and the Peasant

In ancient times, a king had a boulder placed on a roadway. Then he hid himself and watched to see if anyone would remove the huge rock. Some of the king's wealthiest merchants and courtiers came by and simply walked around it. Many loudly blamed the king for not keeping the roads clear, but none did anything about getting the stone out of the way.

Then a peasant came along carrying a load of vegetables. Approaching the boulder, the peasant laid down his burden and tried to move the stone to the side of the road. After much pushing and straining, he finally succeeded. After the peasant picked up his load of vegetables, he noticed a purse lying in the road where the boulder had been. The purse contained many gold coins and a note from the king indicating that the gold was for the person who removed the boulder from the roadway. The peasant learned what many of us never understand. Every obstacle presents an opportunity to improve our condition.

"Success is not a destination, it's a journey."

— Robert Louis Stevenson

"We were together.
I forget the rest."

— Walt Whitman

"Life is what happens
when you are making other plans."

— John Lennon

"If you had a chance to change your fate in life, would you?"

— Brave, the movie

"WHOEVER IN MIDDLE AGE ATTEMPTS TO REALIZE
THE WISHES AND HOPES OF HIS EARLY YOUTH
INVARIABLY DECEIVES HIMSELF. EACH TEN YEARS
OF A MAN'S LIFE HAS ITS OWN FORTUNES, ITS OWN
HOPES, ITS OWN DESIRES."

— Goethe

"Destiny is not a matter of chance, it is a matter of choice.
It is not a thing to be waited for, it is a thing to be achieved."

— William Jennings Bryan

"Some people make things happen, some watch
things happen, and others wonder what happened."

— Mark Erwin

"We make a living by what we get,
but we make a life by what we give."

— Winston Churchill

"Pray as though everything depended on GOD;
work as though everything depended on YOU."

— St. Augustine

"If you want to achieve, associate with those who already have.
If you want to be a winner, be with winners."

— Mark Erwin

"If you don't scale the mountain
you won't see the view."

— Chinese proverb

"If someone gives you a gold mine, you've still got to dig it out."

— Gene Whitley

"Do not go where the path may lead; go instead
where there is not a path and leave a trail."

— Ralph Waldo Emerson

"Reach high, for stars lie hidden in our soul.
Dream deep, for every dream precedes the goal."

— Pamela Vaull Starr

"We write our own destiny. We become what we do."

— Madame Chiang Kai-Shek

"Great thoughts speak only to the thoughtful mind. But the great action speaks to all mankind."

— Emily Bissell

"The harder we try, the luckier we are."   — Sound advice

"ONE WHO FEARS FAILURE LIMITS HIS WORTH. FAILURE IS THE OPPORTUNITY TO BEGIN AGAIN MORE INTELLIGENTLY."

— Henry Ford

"The only person who likes an excuse is the one giving it."

— George Carlin

"The most important things in life are simple but not easy."

— Mark Erwin

"If a man does not keep pace with his companions, perhaps it is because he hears a different drummer. Let him step to the music which he hears however measured or far away."

— Henry David Thoreau

"Adversity is the diamond-dust
that the universe uses to polish its brightest stars."

— Thomas Carlyle

"If you think you are too small and insignificant
to make a difference, you have never spent the night
with a mosquito in your tent."

— Dale Hansen Burke

**"TO TRAVEL HOPEFULLY
IS A BETTER THING THAN TO ARRIVE,
AND THE TRUE SUCCESS IS TO LABOR."**

— Robert Louis Stevenson

"There is plenty of time, but each moment counts."

— Billy Graham

"Act as though it were impossible to fail."

— Dorthea Brande

"It's a funny thing about life: If you refuse to accept anything
but the very best you will very often get it."

— W. Somerset Maugham

"The best way to grow as a person
is to surround yourself
with people smarter than you."

— Mark Erwin

"If you add value to others it will in turn add value to you."

— Mark Erwin

"GENEROUS WILL TAKE YOU FURTHER IN LIFE THAN CHEAP."

— Mark Erwin

"To ignore the facts does not change the facts."

— Milton Friedman

"Arithmetic is not an opinion."

— Caroline Myss

"Winning isn't everything – wanting to is!"

— Arnold Palmer

A Blind Man's Profession

"Painting is a blind man's profession.
He paints not what he sees,
but what he feels, what he tells himself
about what he has seen."

— *Picasso*

"The artist must be in his work as God is in creation."

— *Gustave Flaubert*

"In order to accomplish the impossible,
you must first see the invisible."

— *David Murdock*

"One's art goes as far and as deep as one's love goes."

— Andrew Wyeth

"You use a glass mirror to see your face.
You use works of art to see your soul."

— George Bernard Shaw

"THE MOMENT ONE GIVES CLOSE ATTENTION
TO ANYTHING, EVEN A BLADE OF GRASS,
IT BECOMES A MYSTERIOUS, AWESOME,
INDESCRIBABLY MAGNIFICENT WORLD IN ITSELF."

— Henry Miller

"Imagination is more important than knowledge."

— Einstein

"Nothing happens unless first a dream."

— Carl Sandburg

"Art is man's expression
of his joy in labor."

— William Morris

"At times I can almost feel the presence
of my ancestors – a gently guiding touch
from those who've gone before."

— Bob Timberlake

*"The farther backward you can look,
the farther forward you are likely to see."*

— *Winston Churchill*

"But our existence is in the past, as well as in the future.
Unless we know very well where we have been,
we cannot see where we are going."

— *Charles Kuralt*

"Live as if you were to die tomorrow.
Learn as if you were to live forever."

— *Mahatma Gandhi*

"I must study politics and war, that my sons may have liberty to study
mathematics and science, in order to give their children a right
to study painting, poetry, and music."

— *John Adams*

"To educate the mind and not the morals is to educate a menace to society."

— *Theodore Roosevelt*

"My best friend is a person who will give me a book I have not read."

— *Abraham Lincoln*

"The best use of life is to spend it for something that outlasts life."

— William James

"Painting is silent poetry."

— Plutarch

"A teacher affects eternity; he can never tell where his influence stops."

— Henry Brooks Adams

"He who can reach a child's heart, can reach the world's heart."

— Rudyard Kipling

"CHILDREN HAVE NEVER BEEN VERY GOOD AT LISTENING TO THEIR ELDERS, BUT THEY HAVE NEVER FAILED TO IMITATE THEM."

— James Baldwin

"If you want your children to turn out well, spend twice as much time with them, and half as much money."

— Abigail Van Buren

"What a mother sings to the cradle goes all the way down to the coffin."

— Henry Ward Beecher

"The best classroom in the world is at the feet of an elderly person."

— Andy Rooney

"The great aim of education is not knowledge but action."

— Herbert Spencer

"LEARNING IS NOT ATTAINED BY CHANCE;
IT MUST BE SOUGHT FOR WITH ARDOR
AND ATTENDED TO WITH DILIGENCE."

— Abigail Adams

"The more you know,
the less you need."

— Aboriginal saying

"When man realizes that he is a creative power, and that he may command the hidden soil and seeds of his being out of which circumstances grow, he then becomes the rightful master of himself."

— James Allen

"It is art that makes life, makes interest, makes importance, and I know of no substitute whatever for the force and beauty of its process."

— Henry James

"Art is man's nature; nature is God's art."

— Phillip James Bailey

"Art washes from the soul the dust of everyday life."

— Picasso

"A true understanding of art comes primarily from a true appreciation and reverence for life. No academic study of art can possibly help one to care much for it until he has first been stirred by a love of all existing things."

— N. C. Wyeth

"Anyone who keeps
the ability
to see beauty
never grows old."

— Franz Kafka

One Touch of Nature

"One touch of nature makes the whole world kin."

— William Shakespeare

"The voice of the sea speaks to the soul."

— Kate Chopin

"Our lives are like pebbles on a pond. Some make a big splash and the ripples go deep and far – others only make a slight motion on the surface. No matter how big or small the ripples, the pond soon swallows them all and goes on about its business."

— Mark Erwin

"Science . . . tells us that nothing in nature, not even the tiniest particle, can disappear without a trace. Nature does not know extinction. All it knows is transformation . . . and everything science has taught me . . . strengthens my belief in the continuity of our spiritual existence after death. Nothing disappears without a trace."

— Wernher von Braun

"All I have seen teaches me to trust the Creator of all I have not seen."

— Ralph Waldo Emerson

"My dogs are not just pets, they're family."

— Bob Timberlake

"WE ARE NOT HUMAN BEINGS HAVING
A SPIRITUAL EXPERIENCE.
WE ARE SPIRITUAL BEINGS HAVING
A HUMAN EXPERIENCE."

— Pierre Teilhard de Chardin

"A lack of respect for all living things
soon leads to a lack of respect for humans."

— Luther Standing Bear

"THERE'S A MAGICAL TIE TO THE LAND OF OUR HOME,
WHICH THE HEART CANNOT BREAK,
THOUGH THE FOOTSTEPS MAY ROAM."

— Eliza Cook

"Nothing is worth more than this day."

— Goethe

"A SPORTING LIAR IS A TRUTHFUL MAN TURNED DISHONEST BY CIRCUMSTANCES BEYOND HIS CONTROL."

— *Robert Ruark*

"It's God's land. We are only caretakers for a brief period."

— *Bob Timberlake*

"Many men go fishing their whole lives
without knowing that it is not fish
that they are after."

— Henry David Thoreau

"As no man is born an artist, so no man is born an angler."

— Isaak Walton

FLY FISHING

I hitch up my waders / Step into the cold river
Let out some line / Gather up the slack
Pull my rod back / Snap my wrist
And catch . . . a pine.

— Kristine George

"The broken robin's egg, the forest floor, all bring my thoughts to nature's way: was this only a jay's meal – or the birth of a wondrous new life?"

— Bob Timberlake

"Men in their generations are like the leaves of the trees. The wind blows and one year's leaves are scattered on the ground; but the trees burst into bud and put on fresh ones when spring comes round."

— Homer

"A bird doesn't sing because it has an answer; it sings because it has a song."

— Joan Walsh Anglund

"Happiness consists of a little fire,
a little food, and an immense quiet."

— Ralph Waldo Emerson

"We no longer recognize silence for what it is,
what it does, or why it is necessary."

— Jack Keilpa

"Just remaining
quietly in the
presence of God,
listening to Him,
being attentive to Him,
requires a lot of courage
and know-how."

— Thomas Merton

"THEY DO NOT DIE, THE HOMEPLACES
OF THE SOUTH. THEY HAVE LIVES
OF THEIR OWN AS VIVID
AND TENACIOUS AS KUDZU."

— *Anne Rivers Siddons*

"It all started in a garden."

— *Bob's favorite saying*

"A garden is a place where little miracles occur every moment."

— *Sue Muszala*

"In the wild, the strongest, the showiest, and the sneakiest get the girl."

— *Mark Erwin*

I THINK THE LIFE CYCLE is all backwards. ❡ You should start out dead; just get it right out of the way. ❡ You wake up in a senior care facility and start feeling better every day. ❡ You get kicked out of there for being too healthy, go collect your pension, and then, when you start work, you get a gold watch on your first day. ❡ You work forty years until you're young enough to enjoy your retirement. ❡ You drink alcohol, you party, you're generally promiscuous, and you get ready for high school. ❡ After high school, you go to primary school, you become a kid, you play or nap all day, and you have no responsibilities. ❡ You become a baby with no cares whatsoever. ¶ Then you spend your last nine months floating peacefully with luxuries like spa treatments and room service, and you finish off as an orgasm! ¶ It would be so much better that way.

— George Carlin

"Jonquils are a promise that spring
is just around the corner.
Everything is waking up."

— Bob Timberlake

"I enjoy walking on the beach
and finding all kinds of colorful treasures
left by the tides."

— Bob Timberlake

THE PRACTICE OF SLAVERY EXISTED among American Indians long before the Europeans refined it. It was not uncommon for members of a tribe – either through war, poverty, or trade – to lose ownership of their lives. Once there was a slave called Chiane, which means flower in the sun. She was born the daughter of a chieftain and by birth was a princess. At the age of fifteen her people lost an important war, which caused a dreadful change in her life. Chiane was sold into bondage and taken to the North Country, where she became the property of the Black Stone people. Day after day, she worked hard only to receive scraps of food. The desert days were hot and the nights cold. One night as she wept, a spirit visited her and promised that one day she would bring joy to people everywhere.

Days later a great drought descended upon the land. The skies refused to cool the scorching desert as people, crops, and animals died. Because Chiane was a stranger in the village she was accused of causing such doom. The medicine man, foreseeing the reaction of his people, took Chiane to the crop fields and begged her to pray. Fearing death, she desperately prayed to the Great Spirit for rain. As Chiane prayed, her crystal-like tears fell gently upon the earth, and it began to rain. The people were so happy they gave thanks to the Great Spirit and adopted her. Chiane's remaining years were blessed with a rewarding life. When she died a tall yellow flower grew where she was buried. The Black Stone people gave the flower seeds to their children. The seeds bloomed into a beautiful flower that springs forth annually. Today it is known as the sun flower.

— *From* In the Valley of the Ancients *by* Lou Cuevas

"Bloom where you're planted." — *A garden's wisdom*

"What is really beautiful needs no adorning.
We do not grind down the pearl upon a polishing stone."

— *From a Satakam*

"I try to paint not just objects or houses or landscapes, but, as best I can, the people and history behind the scene that I am working on. I try to capture the love and emotion that I have for a place or person."

— *Bob Timberlake*

"When one has tasted a persimmon in September – a mistake! In October – a benediction!"

— *Charles Kuralt*

"In a moment of awe, nature aligned
to display her organic beauty
and shine beyond the bounds
of my imagination."

— *Carter Ellis*

"When one has tasted watermelon

he knows what angels eat." — *Mark Twain*

"'Just living is not enough,' said the butterfly.
'One must have sunshine, freedom, and a little flower.'"

— Hans Christian Anderson

"We do not inherit the land from our ancestors;
we borrow it from our children."

— Chief Seattle

"No one can ever bring loveliness
into this world unless he is holding fast
the hand of God."

— Archibald Rutledge

"If you would not be forgotten, as soon as you are dead and rotten,
either write something worth reading, or do things worth the writing."

— Benjamin Franklin

"You are never too old to set another goal
or to dream a new dream."

— C. S. Lewis

List of Illustrations

Kuralt at White's Creek   2–3
Hunting Moon   5
Blue Rocker   6
Lighthouse Window   8
Somewhere in Time   11
Hydrangeas   12
Wood Ducks   14
Summer Berries   17
Morning Sun   18
February at Riverwood   21
Mrs. Edna Shoaf Dorsett   22
Midnight Shadows   25
Wanda   26
Volunteers   27
Fenced Out   28–29
Summer Moon   30
Dan's Cherries   31
Iron Eyes   32
Wild Dog Mushroom   35
Gate Latch   36
Christmas Candle   39
Winter Garden   40
Christmas Cardinal   43
Pride in the Carolinas   44
Dan Melton   46
Zinnias   49
Swan Rig   50–51
Sunnyside   52

111

Ray's Moon 55
High Noon 56
Strawberries for Lunch 59
Halloween 60–61
Midday 62
Cape Fear Lighthouse Site 64–65
Dan's Sun Visor 66
Bald Head Lighthouse 69
Together Again 70
Distant Drums 72–73
Lost 74
Blueberries 77
Grubb's Gazebo 78
Summer Green 81
Route 6 Mocksville 82
The Ritual 84
Fresh Cuttings 86
Luna's Pansies 87
Studio Daffodils 88–89
Captain Charlie's View 90
Gilley's House 93
Indian Summer 94–95
May 97
Grandfather Mountain 98–99
Jason's Hollow 100
Knott's Island Decoys 101
Early Jonquils 102
Sand Tracks 103
Sunflowers 104
October Persimmons 107
Ripe 108–109
detail from Gilley's House 110 (13, 16)